CON [barcode] D0329867

CAREGIVING
A Privilege, Not a Prison

JUNE HUNT

ROSE PUBLISHING/ASPIRE PRESS

Peabody, Massachusetts

ROSE PUBLISHING/ASPIRE PRESS

Caregiving: A Privilege, Not a Prison
Copyright © 2017 Hope For The Heart
Aspire Press is an imprint of Hendrickson Publishers Marketing,LLC.
P. O. Box 3473
Peabody, Massachusetts 01961-3473
www.aspirepress.com

Register your book at www.aspirepress.com/register
Get inspiration via email, sign up at www.aspirepress.com

The views and opinions expressed in this book are those of the
author(s) and do not necessarily express the views of Aspire Press, nor
is this book intended to be a substitute for mental health treatment or
professional counseling.

The information in this resource is intended as guidelines for
healthy living. Please consult qualified medical, legal, pastoral, and
psychological professionals regarding individual concerns.

For more information on Hope For The Heart, visit
www.hopefortheheart.org or call 1-800-488-HOPE (4673).

Printed in the United States of America
010817VP

ear Friend,

Years ago, when my mother was in the throes of liver cancer, I thought back on the impressionable words my good friend Jimy shared with me. For decades Jimy, this intelligent, Christian business man, served as his wife's caregiver during her struggle with multiple sclerosis.

In my early 40s, I asked my friend, "How have you handled this burden, especially with her being bedridden?"

"Oh, June" he responded, "She's not a *burden*. She's a *blessing*!"

I'll never forget his words. His perspective made a huge impact on me. As her disease progressed, I watched his wonderful wife cope with her losses: loss of mobility, loss of speech, loss of independence. With each limiting transition, her caring husband met every need. Even when he had to be out of town for a speaking engagement, he arranged excellent care for his bride. Jimy clearly considered her a *blessing*, not a *burden*.

Then when I was in my 50s, for three weeks my mother was unable to speak. One evening, as I was driving home, I called the home care nurse and asked, "How's Mom?"

"June, your mother has become uncharacteristically 'fidgety'—and even tried to pull out her IV! She hasn't slept for three days." Then she exclaimed

"Oh, no, Mrs. Hunt!"

Whatever it was, I yelled, "I'll be right there!"

Immediately, I made my way to her home and bedside. When my efforts to calm her failed, I kicked off my shoes and climbed into the bed with her—fully clothed. I can still see the scene in my mind. I placed my right arm around her and started singing.

Quickly, her restlessness ceased. As I sang, I kept my eyes on her and she kept her doe-like eyes on me. For hours I sang every song I could think of. She smiled as I sang "What a Friend We Have in Jesus," "How Great Thou Art," and "In the Garden." By the time I got to "It Is Well with My Soul," she was mouthing the words. Eventually, during "Amazing Grace," she placed her head on my shoulder—comforted and still—and finally fell asleep.

That memorable night on my mother's bed—connected by the love we had for the Lord and each other—the ministry of music praising her Savior ministered to her soul. God's love touched us both that night, and I wouldn't trade anything in the world for that precious memory. My mother was not a *burden*—she was a *blessing*.

I've learned that caregiving is a calling to model the care of Christ. As Jesus said, He *"did not come to be served, but to serve, and to give his life as a ransom for many"* (Matthew 20:28).

When you are called to be a caregiver, to find a caregiver, or to help a caregiver, remember that God is your unceasing Caregiver. He says, *"I will be your God throughout your lifetime—until your hair is white with age. I made you, and I will care for you"* (Isaiah 46:4 NLT).

My prayer is that God will use the biblical truths found in this book to give you the help, strength, and hope needed to give and receive care. At those times when you feel legitimately burdened, may God bless you as you receive His care and model His care.

Yours in the Lord's hope,

June

June Hunt

CAREGIVING
A Privilege, Not a Prison

Caregiving is a calling of the highest order.

Caregiving becomes the hands and feet of Jesus in the lives of others. Caregiving pours out the love of Jesus upon the weak and weary. Caregiving reflects the heart of Jesus before the helpless and hurting.

Caregivers are our "unsung heroes," serving selflessly and sacrificially. Caregivers are on stage day and night—but far from the spotlight and applause. Yet the cool cloth placed on the warm brow, the spoonful of soup slipped between two lips—all these acts of kindness are unseen here on earth, but heralded in heaven.

And yet to some, caregiving can feel like a prison, a confining duty that squeezes the joy out of life, that siphons the last drop of emotional energy. This is why caregivers must take care to avoid a crisis. Those who minister to others must be ministered to as well.

Ultimately caregiving is a calling, a calling to model the loving heart of Christ.

> **"And walk in the way of love,
> just as Christ loved us and gave himself up
> for us as a fragrant offering
> and sacrifice to God."
> (Ephesians 5:2)**

DEFINITIONS

Pansy came to live with her daughter, Becky, and son-in-law, Ziff. She was not even five feet tall, very slender, and always had a gentle smile and kind disposition. Casual and close friends appreciated how Becky and Ziff treated her with the utmost respect and attentiveness, demonstrating loving examples of caregiving.

Becky was surprised at how caring for her mother, who was in her late 80s, dramatically altered her family's life. At times, pulled down by the weight of responsibilities, Becky felt a loss of freedom to participate in activities such as calligraphy and crafts that were personally fulfilling.

For Becky, time seemed to evaporate. There were never enough hours in the day to meet all the needs. She realized her need to establish better priorities for her time and eliminate some activities that were not absolutely critical. Becky trusted that God had given her time to do everything that was essential.

> "There is a time for everything,
> and a season for every activity
> under the heavens."
> (Ecclesiastes 3:1)

When Pansy came to live in Becky and Ziff's home, the whole family became involved in the caregiving process. Many normal activities needed to be scheduled around Pansy because of her medical needs, such as transportation to and from the doctor's office and the administering of medication at the appropriate times. One person could not do it all. One person could not be totally responsible for Pansy 100% of the time and still maintain a sense of healthy well-being.

However, Becky never indicated that having her mother at home was too much of a burden. Instead, her emphasis focused on the privilege of all she learned and how God was using that time in all of their lives and drawing them closer to Him. As Becky sought many ways to help her mother, she experienced the Lord as her help.

"Surely God is my help;
the Lord is the one who sustains me."
(Psalm 54:4)

▶ *Caregiving* is the act of providing emotional and physical support to someone unable to live independently.

▶ *Caregiving* involves a choice of the heart and mind to give needed help to a dependent person.

▶ *Christian Caregiving* is offered in the spirit of Christ's love, compassion, and by those who have committed their lives to Christ.

▶ *Christian Caregiving* is an extension of the ministry of Christ, empowered by His Spirit. Christians are to provide the *care*, but God alone provides the *cure*.[1]

> **"Carry each other's burdens,**
> **and in this way you will fulfill**
> **the law of Christ."**
> **(Galatians 6:2)**

WHAT Does It Mean to Care?

Becky Young felt that serving her mother was a privilege. She expressed her thoughts this way:

> If I am a servant of the Lord, then I don't get to choose where or how or who I serve, He chooses. What I learned is that God gave me more of a servant's heart. I never wanted to be a nurse or a caregiver. I never had a heart for that. It just wasn't me, but through caring for my mother, God built within me a compassion for others that I never had.[2]

Pansy went to be with the Lord at age 92.

For whatever period of time, if God calls you to be a caregiver, then He wants you to become His hands and feet so that as you serve others, Christ is seen in you. And, as you serve others, the very character of Christ is developed through you.

**"If anyone speaks,
they should do so as one
who speaks the very words of God.
If anyone serves, they should do so
with the strength God provides,
so that in all things God may be praised
through Jesus Christ."
(1 Peter 4:11)**

Caring for someone can take on many forms, depending on the relationship in which the care is given. To care means...

▶ To have a personal interest in

▶ To be affectionate toward

▶ To be concerned about

▶ To give serious attention to

▶ To be watchful over

▶ To look out for

▶ To provide for

▶ To keep safe

**"Lord, you understand;
remember me and care for me."
(Jeremiah 15:15)**

We all have a need to feel that we are contributing to others, especially to those who are meaningful to us. This is why Becky allowed her mother do as much as she could for as long as she could. Sweet Pansy would help set the dinner table and later help clean the dishes. She also ironed Ziff's shirts. Eventually, Pansy became so frail, she could only stand about three minutes then she needed to sit down and rest before resuming the ironing. Even though it took her a while to complete the task, this work enabled her to feel like she was contributing to the family and fulfilling the Lord's plan for her.

> "Commit to the LORD whatever you do,
> and he will establish your plans."
> (Proverbs 16:3)

The need for caregiving can begin suddenly with a serious accident or illness or increase gradually with a slow deterioration in health. Likewise, the need for caregiving can be reduced gradually as a patient recovers or the need can end abruptly if a care receiver dies. Both the extent and duration in the levels of care are dependent on various factors.

▶ **Infant/childcare**—meets the needs of otherwise healthy little ones until they outgrow the need for care.

▶ **Acute care**—fills a temporary need to treat a sudden illness or injury until adequate recovery is achieved.

▶ **Respite care**—provides temporary care to allow the primary caregiver a time for relief and rest.

▶ **Special needs care**—addresses temporary or permanent needs, depending on the nature of the disability.

▶ **Chronic illness care**—supplies minimal to extensive treatment, according to the needs of the patient and the progression of the disease.

▶ **Elder care**—escalates over time as the elderly person's needs typically increase.

▶ **Memory care**—generally becomes more intense if cognitive memory problems impact physical health.

▶ **Hospice care**—is designed to be palliative, which focuses on relieving pain, stress, and other symptoms of terminal illness without treating the underlying cause.

Because physical and emotional needs vary so greatly, we need to pray for God's wisdom as to the right type of care to meet the needs of those whose hearts are heavy.

> "For there is a proper time
> and procedure for every matter,
> though a person may be
> weighed down by misery."
> (Ecclesiastes 8:6)

Although Becky never thought she had enough strength to provide the care needed for her octogenarian mother, she began to experience the supernatural strength of Christ, giving her the strength she needed.

Most people in need of caregiving are part of an existing family with different family members meeting needs in different ways. God's plan for caregivers is summed up in the word *repayment*. God is giving you the opportunity to repay your family for the care you once received.[3]

> "If a widow has children or grandchildren,
> these should learn first of all to put
> their religion into practice
> by caring for their own family and so
> repaying their parents and grandparents,
> for this is pleasing to God."
> (1 Timothy 5:4)

▶ **Primary**

- The primary caregiver is often the eldest or most responsible family member who meets needs on a regular basis (*fills the major role of caregiving*).

▶ **Periodic**

- The periodic caregiver is a reliable family member or friend who provides faithful support for the primary caregiver (*initiates help and is usually available when needed*).

▶ Peripheral

- The peripheral caregiver provides marginal assistance according to personal convenience *(comes for occasional visits or outings)*.

▶ Passive

- The passive caregiver denies or seems unaware of the needs and cannot be relied on to give assistance *(often lacks follow-through even when called on)*.

▶ Professional

- The professional caregiver is a paid care provider who usually is not a member of the family *(may or may not be formally educated or trained)*.

WHERE Does Caregiving Take Place?

Mothers care for their newborn babies, and the rewards are smiles, coos and giggles. Parents care for their children as they grow to maturity, and the rewards are hugs, I-love-yous, and thank-yous. Friends care for each other by giving and/or doing, either tangibly or intangibly, and the rewards are likewise. But what about caring for the elderly who can no longer care for themselves, those unable to give back? Caregiving is not about giving to get. Caregiving is simply *giving* because you *care*.

Where or how you provide care depends on many variables. Most of all, selecting quality care should be paramount and should be provided in the most comfortable, familiar surroundings possible, which is typically in the home. But a top priority first and foremost must be safety.

The Bible assures us that the Lord gives peaceful dwellings in safety.

> **"Whoever listens to me will live**
> **in safety and be at ease,**
> **without fear of harm."**
> **(Proverbs 1:33)**

▶ **In-home care**
- Care receiver's home
- Primary caregiver's home
- Another family member's home
- Group care home

▶ **Care facility**
- Hospital
- Rehabilitation facility
- Acute care facility
- Memory care facility
- Assisted-living facility
- Nursing home
- Hospice care facility
- Adult day care facility

When living accommodations need to be chosen, prioritize a restful, peaceful, secure environment.

When considering the need for care, it's important to examine current care capacity and evaluate future care needs. Many variables will factor into the decisions you make. Although your first inclination may be to retreat and pretend there is "no problem," allow yourself to be vulnerable and share your needs and concerns with others. By being candid with your network of friends, family, and spiritual advisers, you may gain invaluable insights. Their love and support will be indispensable in the days to come.

> **"Plans fail for lack of counsel,**
> **but with many advisers they succeed."**
> **(Proverbs 15:22)**

▶ **Consider the living situation.**

- Living arrangements: Can you provide care in the care receiver's home? In your own home? Will potential changes in the person's condition necessitate physical changes in the living situation (e.g., wheelchairs needing wider door openings)?

- Current working conditions: Will you be able to continue to work in addition to being a caregiver?

▶ **Consider present and future medical needs.**

- Current health condition: Does a medical diagnosis affect other aspects of the care receiver's health? Does your own health as a caregiver affect your ability to give care?

- Expected prognosis: What situations and events can you anticipate? Put a plan in place.

▶ **Consider the financial situation.**

- Current financial resources, assets, liabilities: What are the financial needs?

- Current health, life, and disability insurance: Is insurance available to cover expected costs?

▶ **Consider legal matters.**

- Has a will been prepared? Is a living will in place?

- Is a medical power of attorney in place? A general power of attorney? Have decisions and advanced directives been discussed with family?

▶ **Consider medical treatments.**

- Is there a standard course of treatment?

- Is the care receiver willing to participate in clinical trials or studies?

▶ **Investigate agencies that can offer help.**

- If the illness or impairment is military related, contact the Veterans Affairs office as well as Social Security. Your doctor and local hospital might have valuable resources to share.

- Find out if the illness, injury, or impairment is covered under a specialized agency (e.g., the American Heart Association, the Muscular Dystrophy Association, or other disease-specific foundations), and determine if they offer any care assistance.

▶ **Find a support group.**

- Many illness-specific agencies offer group support services.
- Seek the support and experience of others who share your same struggles.

> **"The heart of the discerning**
> **acquires knowledge,**
> **for the ears of the wise seek it out."**
> **(Proverbs 18:15)**

WHAT IS God's Heart on Caregiving?

Care originates with God, who cares for you. Scripture is filled with examples of His loving care and compassion.

> **"The Father of compassion**
> **and the God of all comfort ...**
> **comforts us in all our troubles,**
> **so that we can comfort those**
> **in any trouble with the comfort**
> **we ourselves receive from God."**
> **(2 Corinthians 1:3–4)** ·

Old Testament Examples of God's Care for You

The God of the Old Testament is the same God of the New Testament. Whatever the situation—God knows, God understands, and God provides.

> **"I the Lᴏʀᴅ do not change."**
> **(Malachi 3:6)**

▶ God **knows** your situation.

"I cared for you in the wilderness, in the land of burning heat" (Hosea 13:5).

▶ God **understands** how you feel.

"In a desert land he found him, in a barren and howling waste. He shielded him and cared for him; he guarded him as the apple of his eye" (Deuteronomy 32:10).

▶ God **provides** for your needs.

"For he is our God and we are the people of his pasture, the flock under his care" (Psalm 95:7).

New Testament Examples of Caring for Others

The New Testament abounds with examples of giving care to others. Whether you are a nurse, a parent, a teacher, an employee—whatever your role—caregiving is a calling and comes from the heart—the heart of a servant, a heart of sacrifice, and it follows the heart of the Shepherd.

**"Anyone who wants to be first must be the very last, and the servant of all."
(Mark 9:35)**

▶ **A Caring Servant's Heart**

- Providing for practical needs

"Many women were there, watching from a distance. They had followed Jesus from Galilee to care for his needs" (Matthew 27:55).

▶ **A Caring Sacrificial Heart**

- Providing for physical needs

"He went to him and bandaged his wounds, pouring on oil and wine. Then he put the man on his own donkey, brought him to an inn and took care of him" (Luke 10:34).

▶ **A Caring Shepherd's Heart**

- Providing for protective needs

"Jesus said, 'Simon son of John, do you love me?' He answered, 'Yes, Lord, you know that I love you.' Jesus said, 'Take care of my sheep' " (John 21:16).

CHARACTERISTICS

At 17, she becomes disabled, and her boyfriend—
disappears!

On a hot July afternoon at the lake, this likable
teen dives into the cool water, but instead of
experiencing a rush of refreshment, pain rocks
her entire body. As Joni Eareckson's head hits the
bottom, the impact snaps her neck, leaving her
paralyzed for a lifetime.

But unlike the vanishing boyfriend, Joni eventually
meets and marries the man who will stay by her
side—*devoted*—a man committed to the caregiving
of his wife and willing to serve and sacrifice. But
that doesn't mean Ken Tada never grows weary
or feels negative emotions—because he does.
However, he learns to lean on the One who never
grows weary and whose understanding is endless.

> "Do you not know?
> Have you not heard?
> The Lord is the everlasting God,
> the Creator of the ends of the earth.
> He will not grow tired or weary,
> and his understanding
> no one can fathom."
> (Isaiah 40:28)

Contracting a chronic illness or incurring a life-altering impairment can be compared to experiencing a simultaneous death and birth, being plucked out of a familiar, warm, comfortable world and thrust into an unfamiliar, cold, painful one. Past identity is lost, along with past abilities. Questions answered long ago cry out to be answered again in the context of this "new me" in this "new situation"—in this new world. "Who am I?" "Why me?" "What's my purpose for living now?"

New thoughts produce strange new feelings, overwhelming and all-consuming feelings that create stress—even distress.

> "Be merciful to me, LORD,
> for I am in distress;
> my eyes grow weak with sorrow,
> my soul and my body with grief."
> (Psalm 31:9)

Some thoughts and feelings that often accompany afflictions include…

▶ **Grief due to change in circumstance** (injury, declining health, or advancing age)

- "Something has happened to me and I'm not who I used to be. I've changed for the worse—nothing will ever be the same again."

"I am worn out from my groaning. All night long I flood my bed with weeping and drench my couch with tears. My eyes grow weak with sorrow" (Psalm 6:6–7).

▶ Fearful frailty

- "I no longer have any control over my life, my relationships, my body, or my future. I am helpless, powerless, and at the mercy of my illness."

"Do not worry, saying, 'What shall we eat?' or 'What shall we drink?' or 'What shall we wear?' … But seek first his kingdom and his righteousness, and all these things will be given to you" (Matthew 6:31, 33).

▶ Anger at needing assistance and caregivers, anger at limitations and affliction, anger at myself and even at God

- "Life is unfair. I did not deserve this. It's not right that I have to suffer when other people are strong and healthy and going on with their lives while I am withering away."

"See to it that no one falls short of the grace of God and that no bitter root grows up to cause trouble and defile many" (Hebrews 12:15).

▶ Powerless due to weakness

- "I've become like a helpless infant, unable to do much of anything for myself. And everyone treats me like I can't think for myself either, like I have lost the capacity to reason and problem solve. I no longer have power over any area of my life."

"I saw the tears of the oppressed—and they have no comforter; power was on the side of their oppressors—and they have no comforter" (Ecclesiastes 4:1).

▶ **Humiliation**

- "I've lost all my rights to privacy. I'm not treated with the dignity every person deserves as a special creation of God. My body is no longer my own—I have little say over what happens to me."

"I have been constantly on the move. ... I have labored and toiled and ... gone without sleep; I have known hunger and thirst and ... gone without food; I have been cold and naked" (2 Corinthians 11:26–27).

▶ **Helpless and Hopeless**

- "I am tired of dealing with my illness. I see no hope of ever getting better, no end to my pain, and no good purpose for it. I might as well crawl into a hole and give up on life."

"We were under great pressure, far beyond our ability to endure, so that we despaired of life itself. ... But this happened that we might not rely on ourselves but on God" (2 Corinthians 1:8–9).

Those suffering from the effects of an illness, accident, or aging may experience a wide range of emotional pain connected to their physical condition, just like the righteous saint from the Old Testament, Job.

> **"I am afraid of all my sufferings."**
> **(Job 9:28 NKJV)**

WHAT Tasks Do Caregivers Perform?

Day in and day out, it's often the mundane tasks of daily life that caregivers take on and take over when called on for help. Caregiving centers around the basics of life—food, clothing, and shelter—but it should be more about taking care of those necessities with a kind and gentle heart, going beyond the basics with companionship, comfort, and compassion.

For many, the shorter their time on earth, the sweeter it can be. Sweeter to savor the preciousness of special people when life is coming to a close.

Taking care of another is so much more than performing a mere task. It is responding to a higher calling—a calling to do the work of God with a humble heart for God.

> **"Whatever you do,**
> **work at it with all your heart,**
> **as working for the Lord."**
> **(Colossians 3:23)**

CAREGIVING TASKS

▶ **Personal assistance/daily activities**

- Personal hygiene
- Dressing, bathing
- Cooking, feeding assistance
- Transportation

▶ **Companionship**

- Sitting, talking, and simply being together
- Reading to the care receiver, talking about what was read
- Playing games, cards, and any form of physical exercise
- Listening to music, watching meaningful TV programs, videos, movies

▶ **General housekeeping**

- Housecleaning, laundry
- Personal shopping, errands
- Pet care
- Home maintenance, yard work

▶ **Medical assistance**

- Track vital signs
- Dispense medication
- Wound care
- Physical therapy

▶ **Financial assistance**

- Write checks, pay bills
- Balance checkbook
- Explore investments/financial aid
- Plan and use a budget

Caregivers can feel a sense of resentment, "My work is never done!" Yes, there is always work for you to do—yet realize, you are called "God's handiwork." And before you were born, He prepared you for this meaningful work. Remember, whatever He prepares you to do, He will equip you to do.

**"For we are God's handiwork,
created in Christ Jesus to do good works,
which God prepared in advance
for us to do."
(Ephesians 2:10)**

WHAT ARE Characteristics of Unhealthy vs. Healthy Caregiving?

When caregiving is handled in an unhealthy manner, both the care receiver and the caregiver are negatively impacted. When a caregiver is rushed, pushed, harried, and overwhelmed, the care recipient feels like a burden, a hindrance, and begins to lose hope. In contrast, a caregiver who is dependable, well-rested, and able to serve in a Christlike manner benefits everyone by providing help and giving hope. The Bible speaks about the help God offers: *"With your help I can advance against a troop; with my God I can scale a wall"* (2 Samuel 22:30).

UNHEALTHY CAREGIVING	HEALTHY CAREGIVING
Unreliable care	Dependable care
Rushed care	Planned and scheduled care
Burdened caregiver	Honored-to-serve caregiver
Stressed caregiving	Strength in caregiving
Exhausted caregiver	Well-rested caregiver
Overwhelmed caregiving	Shared responsibilities in caregiving
Martyr-like caregiver	Christlike caregiver

WHAT IS the Prison of Resentment?

"I saw the weariness in Ken's eyes, and those trapped feelings."[4]

During one particularly difficult season of suffering in early 2007, Joni is confined to bed for two months, and Ken must get up repeatedly every night to turn her from one side to the other. As he sits slump-shouldered on the edge of the bed, Joni empathizes with expressions of "I'd feel weary," "I'd feel resentful," and assures her devoted yet dejected husband of her love and prayer support.

Ken and Joni have been married more than 25 years, so negative feelings from confinement in what seems at times to be a prison of resentment are nothing new to them. Joni remembers that first turbulent year of marriage: "that same trapped look, those same weary expressions on his face, that not-looking-at-you—it's where your husband's just there but he's not there. You can see the sour look on his face, that he's somewhere else."

But the couple courageously confront the issues and learn over the years how to best minister to Joni's primary caregiver. And Ken learns that he can trust in God's promise.

**"He gives strength to the weary
and increases the power of the weak."
(Isaiah 40:29)**

Full-time caregiving can be very demanding. Don't be surprised when negative feelings surface. These feelings are a natural result of emotional and physical fatigue. Many caregivers feel there is no escape from their prison of constant responsibility. Yet, this is often the environment God uses to refine our character and turn our hearts toward Him.

> "For you, God, tested us;
> you refined us like silver.
> You brought us into prison
> and laid burdens on our backs."
> (Psalm 66:10–11)

Prison

P HYSICALLY EXHAUSTED .... fatigued

R ESENTFUL ....bitter and angry

I SOLATED ....lonely and misunderstood

S TRESSED ....guilty and torn

O VERWHELMED .... helpless

N EGLECTED ....unappreciated

As difficult as it is for Joni to live with her disability, she believes it's *doubly* hard on Ken, and she's proactive on curtailing a crisis.

"I'm not the only one who needs God desperately. I'm not even the main one. It's my husband, Ken. I know there are times—bless his heart—when he sighs under his breath, 'I can't do this. I can't face another day of giving Joni exercises, getting her dressed, and lifting her into the wheelchair. I've been through this routine countless times. I don't have strength or resources.'"[5]

And so Ken and Joni enlist additional caregivers—those who primarily help with Joni's "get-up" and "go-to-bed" daily regimens. And Ken is urged by Joni to carve out time for himself, to enjoy his favorite hobbies like fishing and spending time with friends. And while he is her primary caregiver, that is not his top post in her life.

"He's not my nurse. He's not my personal care attendant. He's my husband."[6]

> **"The LORD is my strength and my shield;**
> **my heart trusts in him, and he helps me."**
> **(Psalm 28:7)**

In asking yourself the following questions, honestly assess your feelings to determine whether it could be time to seek help.

The Caregiver's Crisis Checklist

☐ Am I easily agitated with those I love?

☐ Am I becoming more critical of others?

☐ Am I having difficulty laughing or having fun?

☐ Am I turning down most invitations to be with others?

☐ Am I feeling depressed about my situation?

☐ Am I feeling hurt when my efforts go unnoticed?

☐ Am I resentful when other family members are not helping?

☐ Am I feeling trapped by all the responsibilities?

☐ Am I being manipulated?

☐ Am I missing sleep and regular exercise?

☐ Am I becoming so overwhelmed that my caregiving is beginning to suffer?

☐ Am I losing myself in the constant demands of caregiving?

☐ Am I too busy for quiet time with God?

☐ Am I feeling guilty when I take time for myself?

If you feel your stress has turned to *distress*, the Word of God says *"Cast all your anxiety on him because he cares for you."* Since He does care, He will empower you to change the behaviors that are hurting you.

> **"Humble yourselves, therefore, under God's mighty hand, that he may lift you up in due time. Cast all your anxiety on him because he cares for you."**
> **(1 Peter 5:6–7)**

WHAT IS Caregiver Burnout?

After caring for a loved one for a long period of time, with no rest, no respite, or no restoration, a caregiver can burn out. The caregiver finally reaches a point of physical and emotional exhaustion.

Every airline safety speech reminds adults to first put on their own oxygen mask before placing one on a child or someone in their care. Likewise, caregivers must take care of themselves before they can take care of someone else.

Failing to do so can result in physical weariness, compassion fatigue, depression, self-neglect, illness, injury, and a compelling desire to quit caregiving altogether!

Jesus urges those who are weary and burdened to...

**"Come to me,
all you who are weary and burdened,
and I will give you rest."
(Matthew 11:28)**

Signs and symptoms of caregiver burnout include:

▶ **Emotional symptoms**
- Anger
- Irritability
- Anxiety
- Depression

▶ **Physical symptoms**

- Headaches
- Insomnia
- Stress
- Susceptibility to illness

▶ **Social signs**

- Withdrawal from the patient
- Distracted attention span
- Less interaction with family
- Increased isolation from friends

Remember, you do not have to do this all on your own. Call for help when you experience these symptoms. The psalmist reminds us what to do when we are hard-pressed in what feels like a tight place.

> "When hard pressed,
> I cried to the Lord;
> he brought me into a spacious place."
> (Psalm 118:5)

CAUSES

"As to my calling, I belong to the whole world. As to my heart, I belong entirely to Jesus."[7]

She is the embodiment of caregiving—clothed in her characteristic white and blue sari, wrinkled hands reaching out to the poorest of the poor. When Mother Teresa dies in 1997, literally hundreds of homes have been established all over the world to minister to the poor and dying, and she truly fulfills her calling: "to give up all and follow Him [Jesus] into the slums."[8]

And as she follows Jesus, thousands follow her, assisting in the noble cause of caregiving, bringing dignity to those so dreadfully deplored. What keeps the compassion behind the caregiving, what drives the determination to doggedly love the "unlovable"? It is the One who Mother Teresa saw reflected on each and every face.

**"So God created mankind
in his own image,
in the image of God he created them;
male and female he created them."
(Genesis 1:27)**

1. **Fear**

   Becoming a caregiver, especially if you've never been one before, can be a daunting task. Fear of making a serious mistake and not having adequate strength or resources to make it through the duration of your loved one's need for care can foster paralyzing apprehension. Wondering what will happen to your loved one if you should become ill also strikes fear in your heart. Face your sense of fear by seeking adequate training and finding secondary sources of care in the event you become ill or are unable to care for your loved one.

   "For God gave us a spirit not of fear but of power and love and self-control" (2 Timothy 1:7 ESV).

2. **Guilt**

   As you try to do everything all at once, caregivers often become burdened by guilt—whether true guilt or false guilt. Do you wonder if your care is "good enough" to meet all of your loved one's needs? Do you feel guilty if you take time for yourself? When based in truth, good guilt motivates you to act, but let false guilt go! Beating yourself up over faults that are imagined or unavoidable is counterproductive. Focus on what you can do, and recognize that sometimes there will be a gap between what you want to do and what you are actually realistically able to do.

"Let us draw near to God with a sincere heart and with the full assurance that faith brings, having our hearts sprinkled to cleanse us from a guilty conscience and having our bodies washed with pure water" (Hebrews 10:22).

3. Depression

When your role changes from one of relationship—such as a spouse, a son, a daughter, or friend—to that of a caregiver, you can become depressed. The life you loved is in the past, and it's difficult to see a hopeful future. Seeing your loved one suffer is sad and distressing, and your capacity to make things better is limited. Remember to seek medical care for yourself when symptoms of depression arise.

"So my heart began to despair over all my toilsome labor under the sun" (Ecclesiastes 2:20).

4. Resentment

Caregivers shouldering most of the responsibility can feel ignored, abandoned, or criticized by those who aren't as actively involved. This can lead to resentment, a natural response, especially for long-term caregivers. Seek to relieve stress through outlets of support and encouragement, such as in a journal, counseling, or a support group.

"Though one may be overpowered, two can defend themselves. A cord of three strands is not quickly broken" (Ecclesiastes 4:12).

5. Anger

Anger is a valid emotional response to fear, frustration, hurt, or injustice. But what you do with that anger is important. Your loved one's illness or disability may have turned your life upside down. Chronic anger and hostility is destructive, and the Bible calls it sin. Rather than avoiding anger and running the risk of expressing it inappropriately, seek constructive solutions to situations that stir your anger. Be assertive but maintain control.

"An angry person stirs up conflict, and a hot-tempered person commits many sins" (Proverbs 29:22).

6. Worry

Worry differs a great deal from concern. Obsessing over what we cannot change causes headaches and heartaches. Instead of focusing on the what-ifs that lead to worry, cast your cares upon the Lord. Do what you can to help, but leave the rest in His capable hands.

"Since you cannot do this very little thing, why do you worry about the rest?" (Luke 12:26).

7. Embarrassment

For many people, life has been turned upside down. You may experience situations that cause embarrassment, humiliation, or shame either for you or your loved one. Unnerving words or unsettling comments, unacceptable behavior or uncontrollable outbursts can lead to embarrassing moments. Set boundaries as necessary, apologize when appropriate, and move on to the next thing.

"While they curse, may you bless; may those who attack me be put to shame, but may your servant rejoice" (Psalm 109:28).

8. Loneliness

Friends and even family may pull back from you simply because they don't know how to interact with your loved one and they don't know how to help you. The demands of disease often hinder people, resulting in their going into hiding rather than jumping in to help. If you feel isolated and alone, try to expand your social circle to include people in similar circumstances. Consider joining a support group of people who know just what you're experiencing.

"Turn to me and be gracious to me, for I am lonely and afflicted" (Psalm 25:16).

9. Grief

Grief isn't limited to death. Losses of any kind can kindle a flame of grief and sadness. Know that these feelings are normal and allow yourself and your loved one to express sorrow. But don't forget to celebrate joyful times as well.

"Even in laughter the heart may ache, and rejoicing may end in grief" (Proverbs 14:13).

10. Defensiveness

People not in your position are certain to have opinions and ideas about what is "best." But don't bristle at the suggestions of others. Take good ideas into consideration and remain calm. What may sound like criticism at first could actually include some good advice. It's easy to feel unappreciated for all that you do—especially if you are a primary caregiver, responsible for the majority of care. Others looking in from the outside may want to give input from time to time, but not necessarily put in any meaningful time. Remember to walk in forgiveness.

"Anyone you forgive, I also forgive. And what I have forgiven—if there was anything to forgive—I have forgiven in the sight of Christ for your sake" (2 Corinthians 2:10).

False Guilt

QUESTION: **"Why do I feel guilty using an outside facility to care for my family member?"**

ANSWER: You could be experiencing false guilt if you assume responsibilities that God does not initiate. You are told to honor your mother and father, but Scripture is not specific on how you should do this.

"'Honor your father and mother'—which is the first commandment with a promise—'so that it may go well with you and that you may enjoy long life on the earth'" (Ephesians 6:2–3).

Feeling Inadequate

QUESTION: "I am doing everything that is expected of me—why am I still feeling inadequate?"

ANSWER: Rather than resting in the Spirit of Christ, you have given control of your life over to the paralyzing *P*s of:

▶ **Perfectionism**—*The Perfect Christian*

- Trying to do all the right things in your own strength

"Not that we are competent in ourselves to claim anything for ourselves, but our competence comes from God" (2 Corinthians 3:5).

▶ **Performance**—*The People Pleaser*

- Seeking the approval and acceptance of others

"So we make it our goal to please him [the Lord] ... For we must all appear before the judgment seat of Christ, so that each of us may receive what is due us for the things done while in the body, whether good or bad" (2 Corinthians 5:9–10).

▶ **Pride**—*The "Fix-It" Mentality*

- Assuming responsibility for that which God Himself intends to accomplish

"When pride comes, then comes disgrace, but with humility comes wisdom" (Proverbs 11:2).

Jesus is the One Mother Teresa sees in the faces of lepers and orphans, the diseased and the dying.

Her caregiving is never caustic, never heavy-handed. She believes every person deserves "the delicate love of God."[10] The woman known as the "saint of the gutters" spends most of her life demonstrating to the world that caregiving is a privilege, not a prison.

In 1950, Mother Teresa starts Missionaries of Charity in Calcutta, India, to minister to the poor. There are 12 coworkers by her side. Now, thousands of nuns minister on her behalf all around the world in orphanages, schools, hospitals, and shelters for lepers. They answer common questions associated with caregiving and obey the call of Scripture.

> **"As God's chosen people,
> holy and dearly loved,
> clothe yourselves with compassion,
> kindness, humility, gentleness
> and patience."
> (Colossians 3:12)**

It is natural for children to mature into adulthood and become more independent, but roles can eventually switch when parents become elderly, begin to suffer health issues, and need care. When roles of dependence reverse, conflict can arise.

CAUSE OF CONFLICT	CHRISTLIKE RESPONSE
Denial of the need for care	Truth that help is needed and available
Anger at loss of independence	Gentle willingness to help
Depressed about need for care	Hope and joy during time together
Grief at losses to come	Compassion and understanding
Vulnerability of being weak	Trust in God to provide strength
Fear of the unknown	Faith in knowing God has a plan

When you fail to set appropriate boundaries in caregiving, the primary problem is often caused by codependency. This imbalance in a relationship is "idolatry"—giving greater priority to a person than to God Himself. God is the One who created you and has a perfect plan for your life. He is the Lord, who loves you and knows how to fulfill you. If you are in a codependent relationship...

▶ Your *excessive care* causes you to compromise your convictions.

▶ Your *excessive loyalty* leaves you without healthy boundaries.

▶ Your *excessive "love"* leads you to say *yes* when you should say *no*.

God alone has the right to have primary rule in your heart and over your life. Any other substitute is simply idolatry.

The Bible says...

"Love the LORD your God with all your heart and with all your soul and with all your strength."
(Deuteronomy 6:5)

Galatians chapter 6 begins with encouragement to gently restore those caught by sin. Then verse 2 says *"Carry each other's burdens,"* and verse 5 says, *"Each one should carry their own load."* Since these two clear-cut directives seem contradictory to each other, which one is true? There is no contradiction—both are true.

▶ **Verse 1**—Gently encourage another person to change from negative behavior, but beware of your own temptation.

▶ **Verse 2**—The Greek word for "burden" is *baros*, which means "weight," implying a load or something that is pressing heavily.[11] When you help carry what is too heavy for someone else to bear alone, your caring response fulfills the law of Christ.

▶ **Verse 5**—The Greek word for "load" is *phortion*, which means "something carried."[12] When you carry what others should carry, you are not wise. You are not called by God to relieve others of the rightful responsibilities they are able to bear, nor are others to take on your God-given responsibilities.

▶ **Conclusion:** Those who are codependent try to get their needs met by carrying loads that others should be carrying. To move out of a codependent relationship, both individuals need to quit trying to be the other person's "all-in-all" and instead encourage each other to take responsibility for their own lives and to live dependently on the strength of God.

"In their hearts humans plan their course,
but the Lᴏʀᴅ establishes their steps."
(Proverbs 16:9)

As baby boomers continue to age, the so-called "sandwich generation" will be caring for children when they may need to begin caring for elderly parents. In the United States alone, nearly 10 million adults over the age of 50 care for aging parents. This is when they should also be planning and saving for their own retirement. From the late '90s through the first decade of the 21st century, the percentage of adult children providing care to a parent has more than tripled. The total estimated aggregate lost wages, pension, and Social Security benefits for providing care is nearly $3 trillion!

Daughters are more likely to provide basic care while sons are more likely to provide financial assistance.

Caregiving may negatively impact both working sons and daughters in terms of being able to continue working as well as the number of hours worked. Some estimate that more than 65% of caregivers to older adults leave the workforce or reduce their work hours, and women are more likely to leave jobs when they begin care.

Working caregivers also report missing opportunities for promotions, travel, relocation, and education due to costs of providing care. Wages and retirement income can also be impacted.

Costs of caregiving aren't limited to finances. Caregivers who help with chores, errands, and household record keeping also pay a price to the detriment of their own personal, family, and leisure time.

Caregivers also report a decline in their own health the longer they provide care. Almost a third of adult caregivers suffer from stress, anxiety, or depression. Clearly, the costs of caregiving are considerable. Yet those who give care have been given a ministry and, therefore, they can have hope and not lose heart.

The Bible says…

> **"Since through God's mercy**
> **we have this ministry,**
> **we do not lose heart."**
> **(2 Corinthians 4:1)**

WHAT IS the Root Cause for Discontentment?

In 1979 Mother Teresa receives the Nobel Peace Prize for her magnificent work among the poor all over the world. But it is evident as the award is being placed in her hands that she prefers the slums to the international stage, and her caregiver's heart cannot be constrained.

"I choose the poverty of our poor people. But I am grateful to receive (the Nobel) in the name of the hungry, the naked, the homeless, of the crippled, of the blind, of the lepers, of all those people who feel unwanted, unloved, uncared for throughout society, people that have become a burden to the society and are shunned by everyone."[14]

It is Mother Teresa's *desire* to be a compassionate caregiver, not her *duty*. Many Scriptures espouse the virtues of self-sacrifice and service.

> "'I was hungry and you gave me something to eat, I was thirsty and you gave me something to drink,
> I was a stranger and you invited me in,
> I needed clothes and you clothed me,
> I was sick and you looked after me,
> I was in prison and you came to visit me.' ...
> 'Truly I tell you, whatever you did for one of the least of these brothers and sisters of mine, you did for me.'"
> **(Matthew 25:35–36, 40)**

THREE GOD-GIVEN INNER NEEDS

We have been created with three God-given inner needs: love, significance, and security.[15]

▶ **Love**—to know that someone is unconditionally committed to our best interest

"My command is this: Love each other as I have loved you" (John 15:12).

▶ **Significance**—to know that our lives have meaning and purpose

"I cry out to God Most High, to God who fulfills his purpose for me" (Psalm 57:2 ESV).

▶ **Security**—to feel accepted and a sense of belonging

"*Whoever fears the* L*ORD* *has a secure fortress, and for their children it will be a refuge*" (Proverbs 14:26).

THE ULTIMATE NEED-MEETER

Why did God give us these deep inner needs, knowing that people fail people and self-effort fails us as well?

God gave us these inner needs so that we would come to know Him as our Need-Meeter. Our needs are designed by God to draw us into a deeper dependence on Christ. God did not create any person or position or any amount of power or possessions to meet the deepest needs in our lives. If a person or thing *could* meet all our needs, we wouldn't need God! The Lord will use circumstances and bring positive people into our lives as an extension of His care and compassion, but ultimately only God can satisfy all the needs of our hearts.

The Bible says…

"The L*ORD* will guide you always;
he will satisfy your needs in a sun-scorched
land and will strengthen your frame.
You will be like a well-watered garden,
like a spring whose waters never fail."
(Isaiah 58:11)

The apostle Paul revealed this truth by first asking, *"What a wretched man I am! Who will rescue me from this body that is subject to death?"* and then by answering his own question in saying it is *"Jesus Christ our Lord!"* (Romans 7:24–25).

All along, the Lord planned to meet our deepest needs for...

▶ **Love**—*"I [the Lord] have loved you with an everlasting love; I have drawn you with unfailing kindness"* (Jeremiah 31:3).

▶ **Significance**—*"'For I know the plans I have for you,' declares the LORD, 'plans to prosper you and not to harm you, plans to give you hope and a future'"* (Jeremiah 29:11).

▶ **Security**—*"The LORD himself goes before you and will be with you; he will never leave you nor forsake you. Do not be afraid; do not be discouraged"* (Deuteronomy 31:8).

The truth is that our God-given needs for love, significance, and security can be legitimately met in Christ Jesus! Philippians 4:19 makes it plain: *"My God will meet all your needs according to the riches of his glory in Christ Jesus."* A distorted belief system is the reason many caregivers feel there is no escape from the confines of external control. It is important to line up your thinking with God's Word—letting His truth set you free.

▶ Wrong Belief

"It's my *duty* to provide care because others expect it of me. I'm determined to endure this responsibility so I won't feel guilty."

▶ Right Belief

"It is my *desire* to provide care because Christ has called me to serve. I have the strength to endure through Christ and the privilege of fellowship with Him."

**"He will also strengthen you to the end,
so that you will be blameless in the day
of our Lord Jesus Christ.
God is faithful; you were called by Him
into fellowship with His Son,
Jesus Christ our Lord."
(1 Corinthians 1:8–9 HCSB)**

Having a genuine relationship with Jesus Christ not only guarantees an eternity in heaven with Him but also empowers you right now for caregiving. God doesn't want you to take on the monumental task of ministering to others on your own. He longs to help you, giving you *His* love, *His* strength, *His* patience toward others.

To begin this relationship, there are *four* spiritual truths you need to know.

FOUR POINTS OF GOD'S PLAN

1. God's Purpose for You is *Salvation*.

What was God's motivation in sending Jesus Christ to earth?

To express His love for you by saving you!

The Bible says, *"God so loved the world that he gave his one and only Son, that whoever believes in him shall not perish but have eternal life. For God did not send his Son into the world to condemn the world, but to save the world through him"* (John 3:16–17).

What was Jesus' purpose in coming to earth?

To forgive your sins, to empower you to have victory over sin, and to enable you to live a fulfilled life!

Jesus said, *"I have come that they may have life, and that they may have it more abundantly"* (John 10:10 NKJV).

2. Your Problem is *Sin.*

What exactly is sin?

Sin is living independently of God's standard— knowing what is right, but choosing what is wrong.

The Bible says, *"If anyone, then, knows the good they ought to do and doesn't do it, it is sin for them"* (James 4:17).

What is the major consequence of sin?

Spiritual death, eternal separation from God.

Scripture states, *"Your iniquities [sins] have separated you from your God"* (Isaiah 59:2).

"The wages of sin is death, but the gift of God is eternal life in Christ Jesus our Lord" (Romans 6:23).

3. God's Provision for You is the *Savior.*

Can anything remove the penalty for sin?

Yes! Jesus died on the cross to personally pay the penalty for your sins.

The Bible says, *"God demonstrates his own love for us in this: While we were still sinners, Christ died for us"* (Romans 5:8).

What is the solution to being separated from God?

Belief in (entrusting your life to) Jesus Christ as the only way to God the Father.

Jesus says, *"I am the way and the truth and the life. No one comes to the Father except through me"* (John 14:6).

"Believe in the Lord Jesus, and you will be saved" (Acts 16:31).

4. **Your Part is *Surrender*.**

Give Christ control of your life, entrusting yourself to Him.

"Jesus said to his disciples, 'Whoever wants to be my disciple must deny themselves and take up their cross [die to your own self-rule] and follow me. For whoever wants to save their life will lose it, but whoever loses their life for me will find it. What good will it be for someone to gain the whole world, yet forfeit their soul?'" (Matthew 16:24–26).

Place your faith in (rely on) Jesus Christ as your personal Lord and Savior and reject your "good works" as a means of earning God's approval.

"It is by grace you have been saved, through faith—and this is not from yourselves, it is the gift of God—not by works, so that no one can boast" (Ephesians 2:8–9).

The moment you choose to receive Jesus as your Lord and Savior—entrusting your life to Him—He comes to live inside you. Then He gives you His power to live the fulfilled life God has planned for you. If you want to be fully forgiven by God and become the person God created you to be, you can tell Him in a simple, heartfelt prayer like this:

PRAYER OF SALVATION

*"God, I want a real relationship with You.
I admit that many times
I've chosen to go my own way
instead of Your way.
Please forgive me for my sins.
Jesus, thank You for dying on the cross
to pay the penalty for my sins.
Come into my life to be my Lord
and my Savior.
Change me from the inside out
and make me the person
You created me to be.
In Your holy name I pray. Amen."*

WHAT CAN YOU NOW EXPECT?

If you sincerely prayed this prayer, look at what God says!

"His divine power has given us everything
we need for a godly life through our
knowledge of him who called us
by his own glory and goodness.
Through these he has given us his very
great and precious promises, so that
through them you may participate
in the divine nature,
having escaped the corruption
in the world caused by evil desires."
(2 Peter 1:3–4)

STEPS TO SOLUTION

"I wrestled daily with the question of who gets me full-time—Muriel or Columbia Bible College and Seminary?"[16]

Robertson McQuilkin's mind churns with the ministry choices before him: *president* of an established theological institution or *caregiver* of a wife whose vitality is being sapped away by the dreaded disease known as Alzheimer's. Robertson knows he can no longer piecemeal his ministry efforts—both deserve far better, both call for total commitment.

His 22 years at Columbia have wrought significant accomplishments, but Robertson has plans for so many more goals and accomplishments. The drawing board is still chock full. And what have so many godly friends and colleagues counseled concerning Muriel? Institutionalization.

But Robertson's 42 years with his wife have produced a deep, abiding love, rooted in a lifetime marriage covenant. And there can be no getting around that oft-quoted phrase in traditional wedding vows: "in sickness and in health ... till death do us part." Yet of even greater significance is this awareness of the presence of God and, therefore, the witness of God when he spoke those binding wedding vows. He knows he has an accountability partner whose name is Jesus Christ.

So, for highly respected Dr. Robertson McQuilkin, the choice is clear—*caregiving* is the higher calling.

"Husbands, love your wives,
just as Christ loved the church
and gave himself up for her."
(Ephesians 5:25)

Key Verse to Memorize

Refuse to give up when caregiving becomes difficult. Remember, God promises to reward you if you persevere.

> *"Let us not become weary in doing*
> *good, for at the proper time we will reap*
> *a harvest if we do not give up."*
> (Galatians 6:9)

Key Passage to Read

Jesus tells us a story that runs the gamut of emotions: cruelty and callousness, comfort and compassion.

LUKE 10:25-37

The Setup

"On one occasion an expert in the law stood up to test Jesus. 'Teacher,' he asked, 'what must I do to

inherit eternal life?' 'What is written in the Law?' he replied. 'How do you read it?' He answered, 'Love the Lord your God with all your heart and with all your soul and with all your strength and with all your mind'; and, 'Love your neighbor as yourself.' 'You have answered correctly,' Jesus replied. 'Do this and you will live.' But he wanted to justify himself, so he asked Jesus, 'And who is my neighbor?'" (Luke 10:25–29).

THE GOOD SAMARITAN

The Story

This good man is the consummate caregiver—the embodiment of the second greatest commandment: *"Love your neighbor as yourself"* (Mark 12:31).

Yet this man from Samaria is an unlikely model of mercy and compassion. The smug, spiritual leaders scorn his kind—these half-breeds called "Samaritans." The self-righteous Jews refuse to associate with those whose Jewishness has been "tainted" with Gentile blood.

However, through a parable, Jesus reveres the unjustly reviled and heralds the Good Samaritan as the actual hero. But first tragedy strikes.

> **"Jesus said: 'A man was going down from Jerusalem to Jericho,**
> **when he was attacked by robbers.**
> **They stripped him of his clothes, beat him and went away, leaving him half dead.'"**
> **(Luke 10:30)**

The man lay naked, beaten, *half dead* on the treacherous 15-mile road from Jerusalem to Jericho. Adding insult to injury, he proves to be a victim of heartlessness twice more.

▶ *A priest* traveling down the road sees the helpless man and *"passed by on the other side"* (Luke 10:31).

▶ *A Levite*, an assistant to a priest, also sees the obvious, yet *"passed by on the other side"* (Luke 10:32).

These two men—called to minister to the hurting—defy their duty and walk right by. *"But a Samaritan, as he traveled, came where the man was; and when he saw him, he took pity on him"* (Luke 10:33).

"He went to him and bandaged his wounds, pouring on oil and wine."
(Luke 10:34)

As the final bandage covers welts and bruises, the Samaritan could have stood up and strode off down the road, considering his "good deed" complete. But instead his *care continues*.

He places the man on his donkey and takes him to an inn where he further ministers to him. The next day, caregiving takes on an added dimension with the Samaritan meeting the man's *financial needs* as well.

"The next day he took out two denarii and gave them to the innkeeper."
(Luke 10:35)

Two silver coins and a set of instructions signal that an additional level of caregiving is underway.

"Look after him," the Samaritan charges the innkeeper, *"and when I return, I will reimburse you for any extra expense you may have"* (Luke 10:35). The Samaritan enlists the aid of another caregiver in ministering to the man in need.

The Samaritan's caregiving is both *comprehensive* (meeting physical, emotional, and financial needs) as well as *constant* (ensuring the incapacitated man's needs are continually met). The heart of God is reflected in the heart of the Samaritan—the *Good Samaritan.*

To demonstrate His command that you must *"Love your neighbor as yourself "* (Luke 10:27), Jesus tells His story of the Good Samaritan. With an illustration intended to break through the legalistic thinking of the Pharisees, Jesus paints a picture of Love vs. Law.

The Significance

Jesus asks the religious ruler...

> **"'Which of these three do you think**
> **was a neighbor to the man who fell**
> **into the hands of robbers?'**
> **The expert in the law replied,**
> **'The one who had mercy on him.'**
> **Jesus told him, 'Go and do likewise.'"**
> **(Luke 10:36–37)**

The Heart of Caregiving

▶ Have a heart that feels compassion for another. (verse 34)

▶ Have a heart that is willing to give up personal time and resources for another. (verse 34)

▶ Have a heart that ministers to another's physical needs. (verse 34)

▶ Have a heart that provides financial support to another. (verse 35)

▶ Have a heart that includes and requires accountability from others. (verse 35)

▶ Have a heart that remains committed over time to another. (verse 35)

When you feel your strength slipping in your caregiving, remember that you have a Savior who will provide you with the strength to patiently persevere. His Word will revive and restore you so that you can continue to be His precious provider of care. As the Good Samaritan said to the innkeeper, *"Look after him"* (Luke 10:35), how much more will God "look after" and equip you as you do what He has called you to do?

Dr. Robertson McQuilkin recalls the day it all started and traces the steady descent.

Ten years prior: He and Muriel are vacationing with another couple when she repeats a story she had just told five minutes earlier. *That's a first,* Robertson observes. Eventually, activities that come so naturally for Muriel, like entertaining at home and painting portraits, are met with increasing frustration. Her growing inability to process thoughts and clearly communicate soon forces the cancellation of her popular morning radio program and curtails the remainder of her public ministry. "It was a slow dying for me to watch the vibrant, creative, articulate person I knew and loved gradually dimming out," Robertson recalls.[17]

But by Muriel's side he remains.

To overcome overdoing, "dos and don'ts" govern Robertson's management of his wife's disease. *He does* draw upon the Lord's resources for strength, enlist counsel and help from others, and find amusement by watching Muriel pick flowers anywhere and everywhere outside and filling the house with them.

He doesn't resent serving as Muriel's primary caregiver, turn a deaf ear to spiritual lessons being taught along the way, or repress his true feelings that he bears a "subterranean grief" that will not subside.[18]

MY PERSONALIZED PLAN

God is just as concerned about you, the caregiver, as He is about the one placed in your care. If you have a sincere desire to help others, the tendency is to assume too much responsibility and to overdo! Thus, you, as God's chief instrument of care, can become disappointed, depressed, and defeated. Overcome your desire to overdo by developing a respect for these practical dos and don'ts of caregiving.[19]

Dos and Don'ts of Caregiving

▶ **Don't** do everything for the person you are taking care of because it could enable them to the point of becoming prematurely and consequently dependent on you.

   Do encourage personal accountability by asking the care receiver what they want to or think they can do on their own.

   Do share responsibility whenever possible with other family members and friends.

   "For each one should carry their own load" (Galatians 6:5).

▶ **Don't** think you have to have all the answers.

   Do listen carefully for hurts and feelings that are being expressed.

   Do learn to reflect their hurts and feelings so they know you really "hear" and understand what they are expressing.

"To answer before listening—that is folly and shame" (Proverbs 18:13).

▶ **Don't** think you must control people and circumstances.

> **Do** submit to the leading and control of the Holy Spirit.

> **Do** recognize that God has His purposes to accomplish.

"The LORD will fulfill his purpose for me" (Psalm 138:8 ESV).

▶ **Don't** take things too seriously.

> **Do** focus on the positives of the situation.

> **Do** share humorous stories or sayings with the care receiver.

"A cheerful heart is good medicine, but a crushed spirit dries up the bones" (Proverbs 17:22).

▶ **Don't** think your identity is found in meeting another's needs—to do so can quickly develop into codependency.

> **Do** know that you can trust God to meet the needs of others, apart from you.

> **Do** realize that your identity is in Christ.

"For you died, and your life is now hidden with Christ in God" (Colossians 3:3).

▶ **Don't** repress your feelings of hurt and frustration.

> **Do** share your pain with a trusted friend.

Do pour out your heart to the Lord.

"Trust in him at all times, you people; pour out your hearts to him, for God is our refuge" (Psalm 62:8).

▶ **Don't** let yourself become physically exhausted. Lack of rest is a setup for emotional vulnerability.

   Do set aside time to be alone—to exercise, pray, and do whatever revives and restores your spirit.

   Do join a caregivers' support group to receive encouragement and fellowship with others in your situation.

"Because so many people were coming and going that they did not even have a chance to eat, he said to them, 'Come with me by yourselves to a quiet place and get some rest.' So they went away by themselves in a boat to a solitary place" (Mark 6:31–32).

▶ **Don't** become isolated from family and friends for long periods of time.

   Do keep contact with others to help you maintain a positive perspective.

   Do bring other trusted people into the care environment who can bring joy, laughter, encouragement, and hope.

"The pleasantness of a friend springs from their heartfelt advice" (Proverbs 27:9).

▶ **Don't** become spiritually depleted.

> **Do** thank God regularly for His blessings. Call on Him to give you strength when you are feeling weak.

> **Do** increase the amount of time you spend in God's Word to gain hope and encouragement for the long haul.

"'My [Jesus'] grace is sufficient for you, for my power is made perfect in weakness.' Therefore I [Paul] will boast all the more gladly about my weaknesses, so that Christ's power may rest on me. That is why, for Christ's sake, I delight in weaknesses, in insults, in hardships, in persecutions, in difficulties. For when I am weak, then I am strong" (2 Corinthians 12:9–10).

▶ **Don't** try to do it all alone.

> **Do** ask for help from family and friends or engage an outside support person.

> **Do** start each morning with a devotion and prayer with the care receiver.

"The Lord said to Moses: 'Bring me seventy of Israel's elders who are known to you as leaders and officials among the people. Have them come to the tent of meeting, that they may stand there with you. I will come down and speak with you there, and I will take some of the power of the Spirit that is on you and put it on them. They will share the burden of the people with you so that you will not have to carry it alone'" (Numbers 11:16–17).

▶ **Don't** expect to please everyone.

Do accept the fact that others will misunderstand and even be angry with you at times.

Do be led by God's Spirit and seek to do that which pleases the Lord.

"Whatever you do, whether in word or deed, do it all in the name of the Lord Jesus, giving thanks to God the Father through him" (Colossians 3:17).

▶ **Don't** assume a load of false guilt if you have to choose another source of care.

Do evaluate whether you are carrying guilt and, if so, is it true guilt or false guilt?

Do be content that God knows the intent of your heart.

"The LORD said to Samuel, 'Do not consider his appearance or his height, for I have rejected him. The LORD does not look at the things people look at. People look at the outward appearance, but the LORD looks at the heart'" (1 Samuel 16:7).

Various studies that look at the health of caregivers have shown increased rates of clinical depression, anxiety, and other health problems.

Our minds and bodies are intricately connected. Being stressed out or overburdened, if not alleviated, eventually leads to negative physical and emotional changes. Dr. Charles Atkins describes the possible consequences to continual stress.

When chronically stressed, we produce more "stress hormones", adrenalin and cortisol, which over time can lead to medical conditions including hypertension, elevated cholesterol, depression, and anxiety. All of these increase our overall risk of coronary artery disease, heart attack, and stroke.[20]

Let's face it—caregiving is stressful. And being a caregiver for someone with a chronic illness, degenerative disease, or disability can be especially stressful, even to the point of burnout. If you're a caregiver, it may be time to stop, take stock, and de-stress as the Bible suggests.

> **"I keep my eyes always on the LORD.**
> **With him at my right hand,**
> **I will not be shaken."**
> **(Psalm 16:8)**

Caregiver Stress Check[21]

How close are you to burnout? Find out by answering each of the following questions with a *yes* or *no*.

ARE YOU...

☐ In denial about the disease and its effect on the person who's been diagnosed?

"I know Mom is going to get better."

☐ Angry at the person you are caring for, angry that no cure exists, or that people don't understand what's happening?

"If he asks me that one more time, I'll scream!"

☐ Withdrawing socially from friends and activities that once brought you pleasure?

"I don't care about getting together with the neighbors anymore."

☐ Anxious about the future?

"What happens when he needs more care than I can provide?"

☐ Feeling so depressed that your spirit is broken and you feel totally unable to cope?

"I just don't care anymore."

☐ So exhausted that it makes it nearly impossible to complete daily tasks?

"I'm too tired for this."

- ☐ Sleepless due to a never-ending list of concerns?

  "What if she wanders out of the house or falls and hurts herself?"

- ☐ Irritable and moody, which triggers negative responses and actions in you?

  "Leave me alone."

- ☐ Unable to concentrate, making it difficult to perform familiar tasks?

  "I was so busy, I forgot we had an appointment."

- ☐ Experiencing health problems that are taking a mental and physical toll?

  "I can't remember the last time I felt good."

Are you so overwhelmed by taking care of someone else that you neglect your own physical, mental, and emotional well-being? If you find yourself without time to take care of your own needs, you may be putting yourself and your health at risk.

Figuring out how to balance the responsibilities of caregiving with "the rest of life" will always prove challenging. You may be tempted to look outward for the answers to the daily dilemmas your life of caregiving throws at you. Or maybe your first approach is to look inward, hoping to find the energy reserve you need to meet a myriad of daily demands. But God wants you to look upward, to Him.

Release your heavy load to the Lord and allow His peace to permeate your heart.

> **"A heart at peace gives life to the body."**
> **(Proverbs 14:30)**

Ten Ways to Be a Healthier Caregiver[22]

1. **Understand what's happening to your loved one as early as possible.**

   - Don't explain away the changing or unusual behaviors you observe in someone who otherwise seems physically healthy.

   - Consult a doctor when you see changes in memory, mood, or behavior in your loved one.

- Don't wait. Some disease symptoms are treatable.

2. **Know what community resources are available.**

   - Contact local health resources in your community.
   - Visit adult day programs, look into in-home assistance, research visiting nurses programs and meal delivery services.
   - Don't forget to connect with resources at your church. Help may be only a phone call away.

3. **Become an educated caregiver.**

   - Be proactive in learning about your care receiver's disease.
   - Bookmark websites dedicated to specific diseases or resources and visit them often.
   - Find local programs to help you better understand and cope with behaviors and personality changes that often accompany serious and chronic illnesses.

4. **Get help.**

   - Don't try to do everything yourself. This will leave you exhausted.
   - Seek the support of family, friends, and your church. Let them know what they can do to help.
   - Seek professional help if the stress becomes overwhelming.

5. **Take care of yourself.**

   - Watch your diet, exercise, and get plenty of rest.

   - Have a backup plan. Keep a list of people you can call for help when you've reached your limit.

   - Use reputable online message boards for caregivers and local support groups when you need comfort and reassurance.

6. **Manage your level of stress.**

   - Do not ignore physical problems that develop (blurred vision, stomach irritation, elevated blood pressure) or changes in your own behavior (irritability, lack of concentration, change in appetite).

   - Use relaxation techniques that work for you (walking, stretching, massage, music).

   - Talk to your doctor.

7. **Accept changes as they occur.**

   - Admit when the changing needs of your loved one become more than you can manage alone.

   - Become aware of community resources— from home care services to residential care.

   - Prepare yourself emotionally for any physical transitions you see coming.

8. **Make legal and financial plans.**

   - Put legal and financial plans in place now.

   - Consult a professional to discuss legal and financial issues, including advance directives, wills, estate planning, housing issues, and long-term care.

- Involve the patient and family members in these matters, whenever possible.

9. **Give yourself credit, not guilt.**

- Know that the care you provide does make a difference and keep doing the best you can.

- Don't live with guilt. You may feel guilty because you can't do more, but individual care needs can change as time progresses.

- Do whatever is within your power to ensure your patient is well cared for and safe.

10. **Visit your doctor regularly.**

- Take time to get regular checkups. Be aware of what your body is telling you.

- Pay attention to any exhaustion, sleeplessness, or changes in appetite or behavior you experience.

- Get a seasonal flu shot. Being vaccinated protects both you and the person you care for.

**"Do you not know that your bodies are temples of the Holy Spirit, who is in you, whom you have received from God?
You are not your own;
you were bought at a price.
Therefore honor God with your bodies."
(1 Corinthians 6:19–20)**

As Alzheimer's debilitates Muriel's mental processes, her communication comes only in confusing phrases and words—with the exception of one sentence—"I love you," addressed to her primary caregiver.

And before Robertson makes the decision to quit his post at Columbia, Muriel's love is tragically expressed—*through bloody feet.* She cannot bear to be separated from her husband, so sometimes up to ten times a day she walks, or *runs,* to be by his side at the office.

Yet while rational behavior slips away from Muriel, real love remains with Robertson, as well as a privileged predisposition toward caregiving. "She is such a delight to me. I don't *have* to care for her, I *get* to. One blessing is the way she is teaching me so much—about love, for example, God's love."[23]

And the bloody feet—"I wish I loved God like that—desperate to be near Him at all times. Thus she teaches me, day by day."[24]

Love indeed is a compelling force.

> **"Many waters cannot quench love;**
> **rivers cannot sweep it away.**
> **If one were to give all the wealth of one's**
> **house for love, it would be utterly scorned."**
> **(Song of Songs 8:7)**

Your attitude toward caregiving will determine the type of care you give. When you grow weary, ask God to help you see caregiving not as a prison sentence with no chance for parole, but as a privileged opportunity to be the hands and feet of Jesus to those in need.

Privilege

P RAY to have a servant's heart.

"Dear Father, please give me the desire to meet the needs of others unselfishly, without counting the cost of personal sacrifice."

"Serve wholeheartedly, as if you were serving the Lord, not people" (Ephesians 6:7).

R EALIZE that God has chosen you for a special assignment.

God wants to use you to show His love to another. He wants you to cooperate with Him as He brings growth and maturity into your own life.

"We know that in all things God works for the good of those who love him, who have been called according to his purpose" (Romans 8:28).

I DENTIFY attitudes that may be blocking your ability to respond to God.

"Dear Father, help me to recognize any anger, bitterness, unforgiveness, resentment, hopelessness, pride, and self-pity that reside in my own heart. Make me willing to release these inappropriate attitudes to You and replace them with Your Spirit of love, sincerity, forgiveness, patience, gratefulness, thanksgiving, and joy."

"Create in me a pure heart, O God, and renew a steadfast spirit within me" (Psalm 51:10).

V ALUE this opportunity, for it is only temporary.

"Dear Father, thank You for this opportunity to be Your servant in the life of another person. Please give me the grace to trust in Your perfect timing."

"In all this you greatly rejoice, though now for a little while you may have had to suffer grief in all kinds of trials" (1 Peter 1:6).

I NVEST your life in the life of another.

Build an intimate relationship with the person you are caring for by identifying with their feelings and being vulnerable with your own. Pray for their needs daily.

"No one has ever seen God; but if we love one another, God lives in us and his love is made complete in us" (1 John 4:12).

L EARN to live one day at a time.

Begin each day by talking to God. Stay focused on His presence throughout the day, recognizing that He is orchestrating each event as it unfolds.

"The LORD has done it this very day; let us rejoice today and be glad" (Psalm 118:24).

Exchange your weakness for Christ's strength.

Remember that God's grace is sufficient for anything you will face. Depend on His Spirit to guide you and submit to Him as He prompts even when you don't feel like it.

"I can do all things through Christ who strengthens me" (Philippians 4:13 NKJV).

Give up expectations.

Don't expect others to understand what you are going through or express appreciation for all that you are doing as a caregiver. Let go of unrealistic expectations you have of yourself and the person you are caring for.

"Anxiety weighs down the heart, but a kind word cheers it up" (Proverbs 12:25).

Experience a deeper intimacy with God.

Remember that God is always with you no matter what you and those you love must endure. He will walk with you through every experience of life.

"Where can I go from your Spirit? Where can I flee from your presence? If I go up to the heavens, you are there; if I make my bed in the depths, you are there. If I rise on the wings of the dawn, if I settle on the far side of the sea, even there your hand will guide me, your right hand will hold me fast" (Psalm 139:7–10).

Picking blueberries. Playing games. Singing, cooking, making a quilt *together* are little ways that the McQuilkin family ministers to a wife, mother, and grandmother suffering from Alzheimer's. It is dubbed both a family reunion and a 40th wedding anniversary celebration as the McQuilkins whisk Muriel away to a mountain retreat and express how much she means to them, *before she no longer knows them.*

The occasion is actually the 39th wedding anniversary for Robertson and his wife, but just as great a reality is that no one knows when Muriel will no longer recognize her husband or a single one of her six children. So as a family they savor the "small stuff" and surround a beloved matriarch with the Savior's love.

Muriel struggles with Alzheimer's for 25 years, but her battle finally ends upon her death on September 20, 2003, at the age of 81.

A godly family that gave it all embodies the following Scripture...

**"For we are God's handiwork,
created in Christ Jesus to do good works,
which God prepared
in advance for us to do."
(Ephesians 2:10)**

You may never be called to provide full-time care for a friend, relative, or close family member, but you are always on call to show the love of God in small, meaningful ways to others. It's often the "little things" that bring the most appreciation and joy. Reveal your heart for God by recognizing practical ways to be the good Samaritan in the life of another. Remember—*A little will be much when it's placed in the Master's hand!*

PRACTICAL WAYS FRIENDS CAN GIVE CARE

▶ Send cards and handwritten notes.

▶ Make visits (ask if they should be short or longer ones).

▶ Bring a bouquet of flowers.

▶ Give small gifts.

▶ Bring helpful books, videos, and booklets.

▶ Lift the spirit with laughter—hang humorous posters.

▶ Keep a record of remembrances—put together a scrapbook of pictures.

▶ Provide food and occasionally an entire meal.

▶ Volunteer to provide transportation.

▶ Reach out to the children or other family members.

▶ Shop for needed items—call and ask for a list.

▶ Bring the gift of music—inspirational music CDs.

▶ Set aside time for regular reading aloud.

▶ Offer to meet some personal needs (warm washcloth for face in the morning, assist with brushing teeth, combing hair, shaving, help applying makeup to feel presentable).

▶ Take walks and do other outdoor activities.

▶ Offer to do housework, yard work, laundry, or repairs.

▶ Be a willing and attentive listener.

▶ Extend emotional affection (be an empathetic listener, seek to make a "heart connection," making them feel cherished and valued, and seek to understand their hurts, dreams, longing, regrets, and joys).

▶ Extend physical affection (hand holding, pats on the back, foot rubbing, scalp massage).

▶ Provide financial assistance.

▶ Become a prayer warrior.

> **"God is not unjust;**
> **he will not forget your work**
> **and the love you have shown him**
> **as you have helped his people**
> **and continue to help them."**
> **(Hebrews 6:10)**

There may come a time in the course of your loved one's illness that you must say *no* to caregiving. It may be a temporary *no* in that you need respite care to take your place briefly. It may be a *no* in that you need to withdraw from caring for your loved one so that someone else with more expertise can handle a crisis situation. Or, it may be a *no* in that the time has come for the role of caregiver to be taken over by someone else entirely.

▶ Understanding the reasons behind your *no* is an important first step.

▶ Questions to ask:

- Does your caregiving situation need to change to maintain a meaningful relationship?

- Who is available to take the caregiving task in your stead?

▶ Express caregiving limitations using "I" statements and offer alternative solutions:

- "Dad, I can't continue to drive you to all of your doctor appointments because of my work schedule. Let's look at other options, such as a medical transportation service that can pick you up and drop you off."

- "Mom, I won't be able to keep cleaning your house every week. I'd rather spend the time with you doing other things. I know it will be difficult to let other people help, but let's find a cleaning service you'll like."

- "These stairs are getting difficult for us to manage. I'm worried about your safety and mine. I think we need to build a ramp for easier access, and I've found a carpenter who charges reasonable rates."

Elder Abuse

QUESTION: "What constitutes elder abuse, and what can I do if I suspect an elderly person is being mistreated to the point of it being considered abusive?"

ANSWER: Most cases of elder abuse go undetected and thus unreported, leaving many of those to whom we owe the most feeling devalued, dejected, and demoralized. Elder abuse is usually considered to be both intentional and unintentional acts by a "trusted" person that cause or might cause harm to befall a vulnerable elder. Acts that constitute abuse include:

▶ Abandonment

▶ Emotional or psychological mistreatment

▶ Exploitation

▶ Financial abuse

▶ Neglect

▶ Physical mistreatment

▶ Sexual abuse

Abuse has only to be suspected, not proven, by the person reporting it. Professionals investigating the report are the ones responsible for verifying the legitimacy of the report.

To report suspected elder abuse in the community, call your local Adult Protective Services agency or call the Eldercare Locator at 1-800-677-1116. To report suspected abuse in a nursing home or long-term care facility, contact your local Long-Term Care Ombudsman or call the Eldercare Locator (number recorded above).

The National Center on Elder Abuse (NCEA) at www.ncea.aoa.gov helps communities, agencies, and organizations ensure that elders and adults with disabilities can live with dignity and without abuse, neglect, and exploitation. It provides education, research, and promising practices in stopping abuse.

**"Bring to an end the violence of the wicked
and make the righteous secure—
you, the righteous God who probes
minds and hearts."
(Psalm 7:9)**

HOW TO Set Appropriate Boundaries

Boundaries are necessary in relationships, and that applies to caregiving too. Boundaries are lines that separate acceptable behavior from unacceptable behavior—actions you will tolerate and actions you will not tolerate.

▶ When a boundary is *respected*, the result is a *reward*. God set up a moral boundary for Adam and Eve—a boundary based on right and wrong. When this boundary line was honored, the couple enjoyed the abundance of the garden and unbroken fellowship with God.

▶ When a boundary is *rejected*, the result is a *repercussion*. When this boundary line was crossed, sin entered the world—a repercussion that disqualified Adam and Eve from staying within the bounds of the garden.

When you communicate a clear, rightful boundary—with a reward and a repercussion—and someone violates that boundary, enforcement of the repercussion should be inevitable and at times instantaneous. The violator not only chose to violate the boundary, but also chose the repercussion attached to it.

The principle of rewards and repercussions was clearly demonstrated when God set a boundary with Adam and Eve. In choosing to violate the boundary established by the Lord, they automatically chose the repercussion assigned to their sin.

> "To Adam he said, 'Because you listened
> to your wife and ate fruit from the tree
> about which I commanded you,
> "You must not eat from it,"
> Cursed is the ground because of you;
> through painful toil you will eat food from it
> all the days of your life.'"
> (Genesis 3:17)

One way in which boundaries can be established in caregiving is through understanding that just as patients have rights, caregivers also have rights.

A CAREGIVER'S BILL OF RIGHTS[25]

As a caregiver, you have the right:

▶ To take care of yourself. This is not an act of selfishness. It will give you the capability to take better care of your loved one.

▶ To seek help from others even though your loved ones may object. You recognize the limits of your own endurance and strength.

▶ To maintain facets of your own life that do not include the person you care for, just as you would if your loved one were healthy. You know that you do everything that you reasonably can, and you have the right to do some things just for yourself.

▶ To get angry, be depressed, and express other difficult feelings occasionally.

▶ To reject any attempts by your loved one (either conscious or unconscious) to manipulate you through guilt and/or depression.

▶ To receive, from your loved ones, consideration, affection, forgiveness, and acceptance for what you do, as long as you offer these qualities in return.

▶ To take pride in what you are accomplishing and to applaud the courage it has sometimes taken to meet the needs of your loved one.

▶ To protect your individuality and your right to make a life for yourself that will sustain you when your loved one no longer needs your full-time help.

▶ To support research to find resources that aid the physically and mentally impaired, as well as those in a caregiving role.

Boundaries guard us from giving more than we should and protect us from others taking more than they should. And boundaries make it possible for us to enjoy mutual "give-and-take" within healthy relationships.

**"Above all else, guard your heart,
for everything you do flows from it."
(Proverbs 4:23)**

SCRIPTURES TO MEMORIZE

What will happen to **those who** place their **hope in the Lord**?

> *"Those who hope in the LORD will renew their strength. They will soar on wings like eagles; they will run and not grow weary, they will walk and not be faint"* (Isaiah 40:31).

Who will help us **daily bear our burdens**?

> *"Praise be to the Lord, to God our Savior, **who daily bears our burdens**"* (Psalm 68:19).

As God's chosen people, how are you to **clothe yourselves**?

> *"**As God's chosen people**, holy and dearly loved, **clothe yourselves** with compassion, kindness, humility, gentleness and patience"* (Colossians 3:12).

Who **provides the strength** needed to **serve** others?

> *"If anyone **serves**, they should do so with **the strength** God **provides**"* (1 Peter 4:11).

What is the result if you **serve** people **wholeheartedly**?

> *"**Serve wholeheartedly**, as if you were serving the Lord, not people"* (Ephesians 6:7).

How can you help **fulfill the law of Christ**?

*"Carry each other's burdens, and in this way you will **fulfill the law of Christ**"* (Galatians 6:2).

Who **comforts us in all our troubles** so that we can comfort others?

*"Praise be to the God and Father of our Lord Jesus Christ, the Father of compassion and the God of all comfort, who **comforts us in all our troubles**, so that we can comfort those in any trouble with the comfort we ourselves receive from God"* (2 Corinthians 1:3–4).

Where can I go to find **rest** when I am **weary and burdened**?

*"Come to me, all you who are **weary and burdened**, and I will give you **rest**"* (Matthew 11:28).

Why should I **not become weary in doing good**?

*"Let us **not become weary in doing good**, for at the proper time we will reap a harvest if we do not give up"* (Galatians 6:9).

Who will **understand and care for me**?

*"LORD, you **understand**; remember me **and care for me**"* (Jeremiah 15:15).

NOTES

1. Kenneth C. Haugk, *Christian Caregiving—A Way of Life* (Minneapolis MN: Augsburg Publishing House, 1984), 19.

2. For all quotations and references to Becky Young and her family, see Becky Young in conversation with the author, n.d.

3. Timothy S. Smick, James W. Duncan, J. P. Moreland, and Jeffrey A. Watson, *Eldercare for the Christian Family* (Dallas: Word, 1990), 12–13.

4. For this section, see "Praying Through Football Season," Joni Eareckson Tada, interview by Nancy DeMoss Woglemuth, *Revive Our Hearts Radio*, July 8, 2010, accessed July 14, 2017, https://www.reviveourhearts.com/radio/revive-our-hearts/praying-through-football-season-1/.

5. Joni Eareckson Tada, foreword to *A Caregiver's Survival Guide: How to Stay Healthy When Your Loved One Is Sick*, by Kaye Marshall Strom (Downers Grove, IL: InterVarsity Press, 2000), 9.

6. "Praying Through Football Season," Joni Eareckson Tada, interview by Nancy DeMoss Woglemuth, *Revive Our Hearts Radio*, July 8, 2010, accessed July 14, 2017, https://www.reviveourhearts.com/radio/revive-our-hearts/praying-through-football-season-1/.

7. Mother Teresa at *All Great Quotes*, accessed September 2015, http://www.allgreatquotes.com/mother_teresa_quotes.shtml.

8. Ruth A. Tucker, "Ministries of Mercy: Mother Teresa," *Christian History & Biography*, January 1, 2000, http://www.ctlibrary.com/ch/2000/issue65/4.20.html.

9. Paula Spencer Scott, "The 7 Deadly Emotions of Caregiving," Caring.com, accessed September 2015, https://www.caring.com/articles/7-deadly-emotionsof-caregiving; Lois D. Knutson, *Compassionate Caregiving: Practical Help and Spiritual Encouragement*, (Bloomington, MN: Bethany House Publishers, 2007), 44–46.

10. *CNN.com*, "Mother Teresa's Legacy Knows No Boundaries," http://www.cnn.com/WORLD/9709/05/mother.teresa/index.html.

11. Vine, Unger, and White, *Vine's Complete Expository Dictionary of Biblical Words*, s.v. "burden."

12. Spiros Zodhiates, *The Hebrew-Greek Key Study Bible: New International Version* (Chattanooga, TN: AMG, 1996), 1507.

13. *The MetLife Study of Caregiving Costs to Working Caregivers: Double Jeopardy for Baby Boomers Caring for Their Parents*, June 2011; http://www.caregiving.org/wp-content/uploads/2011/06/mmi-caregivingcosts-working-caregivers.pdf.

14. Mother Teresa at *All Great Quotes*, accessed September 2015, http://www.allgreatquotes.com/mother_teresa_quotes.shtml.

15. Lawrence J. Crabb, Jr., *Understanding People: Deep Longings for Relationship*, Ministry Resources Library (Grand Rapids: Zondervan, 1987), 15–16; Robert S. McGee, *The Search for Significance*, 2nd ed. (Houston, TX: Rapha, 1990), 27–30.

16. Robertson McQuilkin, "Living by Vows," *Christianity Today*, October 8, 1990, 38–40.

17. McQuilkin, "Living by Vows," *Christianity Today*, October 8, 1990, 38–40.

18. McQuilkin, "Living by Vows," *Christianity Today*, October 8, 1990, 38–40.

19. Carol Travilla, *Caring Without Wearing* (Colorado Springs, CO: NavPress, 1990), 67–68.

20. Charles Atkins, *The Alzheimer's Answer Book* (Naperville, IL: Sourcebooks, 2008), 227.

21. *Alzheimer's Association* "10 Symptoms of Caregiver Stress," published by and distributed through a local chapter of the Greater Dallas Alzheimer's Association area support group.

22. *Alzheimer's Association* "How to Manage Stress: 10 Ways to Be a Healthier Caregiver," adapted from a handout distributed through local chapters of the Greater Dallas Area Alzheimer's Association.

23. McQuilkin, "Living by Vows," *Christianity Today*, October 8, 1990, 38–40.

24. McQuilkin, "Living by Vows," *Christianity Today*, October 8, 1990, 38–40.

25. Jo Horne; "A Caregiver's Bill of Rights," *Today's Caregiver*, accessed October 2015, http://caregiver.com/articles/caregiver/caregiver_bill_of_rights.htm.

HOPE FOR THE HEART TITLES

- *Adultery*
- *Aging Well*
- *Alcohol & Drug Abuse*
- *Anger*
- *Anorexia & Bulimia*
- *Boundaries*
- *Bullying*
- *Caregiving*
- *Chronic Illness & Disability*
- *Codependency*
- *Conflict Resolution*
- *Confrontation*
- *Considering Marriage*
- *Critical Spirit*
- *Decision Making*
- *Depression*
- *Domestic Violence*
- *Dysfunctional Family*
- *Envy & Jealousy*
- *Fear*
- *Financial Freedom*
- *Forgiveness*
- *Friendship*
- *Gambling*
- *Grief*
- *Guilt*
- *Hope*
- *Loneliness*
- *Manipulation*
- *Marriage*
- *Overeating*
- *Parenting*
- *Perfectionism*
- *Procrastination*
- *Reconciliation*
- *Rejection*
- *Self-Worth*
- *Sexual Integrity*
- *Singleness*
- *Spiritual Abuse*
- *Stress*
- *Success Through Failure*
- *Suicide Prevention*
- *Trials*
- *Verbal & Emotional Abuse*
- *Victimization*

www.aspirepress.com